THE IRREFUTABLE ROLE OF GATEKEEPERS

Also by Chris Omoijiade

YOU TOO CAN BE DEBT-FREE: A First Hand
Witness Account on the Horrors of Debt

SO YOU WANT TO LEAD

LEADERSHIP GEMS IN THE BIBLE:
(The Old Testament Vol. 1)

LEADERSHIP GEMS IN THE BIBLE:
(The Old Testament Vol. 2)

LEADERSHIP GEMS IN THE BIBLE:
(The New Testament)

GET AHEAD: Practical Steps To Face Life's
Realities and Embrace Success

THE IRREFUTABLE ROLE OF

GATE KEEPERS

TO YOUR SUCCESS
& KEY PRINCIPLES ON
HOW TO WIN THEM OVER

CHRIS OMOIJIADE

The Irrefutable Role of Gatekeepers
To Your Success & Key Principles
on How to Win Them Over

Published by:
ScribeTribe Africa
5, Prince Ibrahim Eletu Avenue,
Lekki, Lagos

www.scribetribe.media
scribetribeafrica@gmail.com
+234 (0) 708 040 1080, +234 (0) 813 527 3602

Distributed by:
The Chris Omoijiade Company
+234 810 950 0000, +234 908 123 0000
ceo@tcocglobal.com
admin@tcocglobal.com
www.tcocglobal.com
chrisomoijiade
Chris Omoijiade
Christopher Omoijiade
Christopher Omoijiade

THE
Chris Omoijiade
COMPANY
SOLI DEO GLORIA

CHRISTOPHER E. OMOIJIADE
SOLI DEO GLORIA

ARIMATHEA
ARIMATHEA BELIEVERS NETWORK

*This book is dedicated to Yahweh,
the I Am, the Holy Father of all spirits
and heavenly lights*

*To Jesus the Christ, Prince of Peace,
the Word and Eternal King*

*And the indispensable
Sceptre of the living Sovereign God,
Spirit of Glory, Wisdom, and Revelation,
the Holy Spirit.*

*I am indeed a product of
undeserved mercy.*

*Thank you, Abba, for
adopting me!*

Acknowledgemnts

I extend my heartfelt gratitude to Apostle Joshua Selman of Eternity Network International (Koinonia Global), for profoundly shaping my philosophy on relationships. Your selfless dedication to imparting practicable and timely wisdom keys has provided a strong foundation for the navigation of the spiritual and personal journey of millions globally. More grace, sir.

CONTENTS

INTRODUCTION

We all live in a world of men. For emphasis' sake, *"WE LIVE IN A WORLD OF MEN."* As such, the success you seek in your earthly sojourn must come through a conduit, and that pipeline is the earthen vessel called man: mortals like you with flesh on their bones and blood in their veins. These vessels who mirror the same emotions that you embody will help you along the way to success.

Many of the individuals, systems or structures that will make your dreams come true can be likened to the immigration officers we see at most international airports on arrival or departure. They have the single job description to control entry and exit into territories. For the purpose of this discourse, I would like to describe them as "gatekeepers".

Over the past few decades, in thousands of interactions with several individuals from all walks of life, especially those who are adjudged successful by earthly standards, it became more evident to me that one of the major reasons individuals struggle to reach the pinnacle of their endeavours is that there is the lack of a methodical compression of principles that individuals can put to work to win men over to their side and have them do their bidding in a non-manipulative manner. Such principles, when backed by scriptural wisdom, shed light on the reasons some men act as barriers instead of door openers.

Gatekeepers play an irrefutable role in your attempt to make your stay in this earthly realm fruitful and worthwhile. This is because everything you "desire", "need" and "want" is in the hands of "other men". Therefore, how you can get past the barriers to reach them is the million-dollar question.

While there is an acknowledgment that all blessings come from above, there is a vital piece of information you must embrace: the blessings of God to men must be routed from the spiritual to the physical through what is termed the ministry of men.

Consequently, we must seek to undertake a thorough archaeological analysis of what principles can make you win over men and, more importantly, have these gatekeepers support your cause. This is one of the best decisions you can make because the absence of the support of men in life and business is guaranteed to produce a very hard and frustrating existence.

The root of many individuals struggling in the throes of poverty, discomfort, lack and limitations can, in many instances, be traced back to their inability to embrace the ministry of men, acquiring the keys to unlock the souls of men, understanding the mindset of such men and getting them to act in a way that lifts them to their desired position.

Thankfully, this book seeks to pull you out of the murky waters of ignorance. In other words, it will guarantee your evolution into a person that other men seek to be a blessing to. Recall that while the role of the spiritual can never be undermined, its efficacy is tied to the actions that you take to see your desire become a reality, resulting in your ascension to greatness.

WHO ARE GATEKEEPERS?

Let's start with what a gate is. You may live in a home or a community, surrounded by gates of different types, all with a common purpose to grant or deny people access. Therefore, a gate can be defined for the purpose of our discourse here as an access point.

By extension, a gatekeeper is the description given to any individual or system who stands in the way between you and key decision-makers or any individual that is responsible for granting you your heart's desires. A gatekeeper is any individual responsible for access through gates.

At the mention of gatekeepers, some of us may, at first, have mental pictures of receptionists, secretaries or administrative assistants whose roles often include the brief to screen unwanted or irrelevant calls from reaching their bosses. Beyond that, it could also be that protocol officer of that man of faith, it may be the aide-de-camp of that government officer and it may be that personal assistant of that CEO of a major corporation. Such individuals are human guards, and they often act as a hurdle to both individuals and doors. In our very busy modern world, they act as a buffer, ready to weed out irrelevant activities and prevent them from proceeding to their principals or a place of opportunity.

In the case of being hurdles to key decision-makers or offices, such individuals wield greater influence than most individuals realize and boast of busy schedules that make time a limited resource. It is incredibly important for them to keep their businesses running efficiently and smoothly. Therefore, these gatekeepers act as a shield, protecting individuals, systems and structures from unwanted distractions or potential time wasters who offer no value, or who might distract them from their main responsibilities.

These human doors can either choose to help or frustrate fellow men. You must keep in mind that, whatever access you are looking for, there are hundreds and possibly thousands looking for the same. Whether it is access to individuals, systems or even structures, most individuals fall a step short of their desired targets, with their inability to win over powerful gatekeepers.

I cannot overemphasize this: gatekeepers are very important to your life, to your success and, most importantly, to your destiny. They will be found in every place men congregate: in the workplace, government, service, religion, business circles and everywhere you need something or someone.

Unfortunately, many have not paid the all-important price of mental transformation in dealing with men, conveniently forgetting or just ignorant of the principles to be adopted that will change their attitudes, train them to treat others well and, in the process, achieve their set goals.

You can choose to finally put off the garment of struggle with men when you learn the principles that are imperative to win and keep men, thus making the principles a way of life. In the following chapters are life principles gleaned from Scripture and life experiences that offer you, the reader, unique perspectives on how you can win over gatekeepers that play an irrefutable role in your success in life and business.

KEY PRINCIPLES ON HOW TO WIN OVER GATEKEEPERS

FAVOUR

"Later when King Xerxes fury had subsided,
he remembered Vashti and what she had done and what he
had decreed about her. Then the King's personal attendants proposed,
let a search be made for beautiful young virgins for the king.
Let the King appoint commissioners in every province of his realm
to bring all these beautiful young women into the harem at the
citadel of Susa. Let them be placed under the care of Hegai,
the king's eunuch, who is in charge of the women; and let beauty
treatments be given to them. Then let the young woman who
pleases the king be queen instead of Vashti."
Esther 2:1-4 (NIV)

"When the King's order and edict had been proclaimed
many young women were brought to the citadel of Susa
and put under the care of Hegai. Esther also was taken to the
king's palace and entrusted to Hegai, who had charge of the harem.
**She pleased him and won his favour. Immediately he provided
her with beauty treatments and special food. He assigned to
her seven female attendants selected from the king's palace,
and moved her and her attendants into the
best place in the harem."**
Esther 2:8-10 (NIV)

Esther was a young countryside girl nominated by her uncle Mordecai for the ultimate beauty pageant of the time, with the grand prize of becoming the queen to the great Persian King Xerxes who, in fury, had put away his previous queen. Her offence was her refusal to entertain the king and his guests at a banquet, an action the king found demeaning. It undermined his authority, potentially causing a dent in his reputation and his royal ego.

A royal decree was subsequently issued by the royal court, and the most beautiful damsels were recruited into the harem of the king to undergo a rigorous and lengthy year-long preparation, where they would be pampered with the best beauty treatments.

In the midst of all of these, there was a divine move by the Almighty God to position Esther to be queen to save the children of Israel, but there was a certain man, Hegai, whom we could call a gatekeeper of King Xerxes. His foreknowledge of the king, including his likes and desires, was a cheat code for any of the ladies in contention for the crown.

Therefore, the most important thing that any of the aspiring maidens needed for access was "favour", which is described as an act of kindness beyond what is due or usual, in order to win this gatekeeper. And that is what Esther got. In my personal dealings with men, and I am sure in your own individual life too, you might have come across situations when you received that favour that seemed to push you right in front of the queue, breaking protocol. You observed scripts re-written just for your sake. Such events have one important catalyst which is favour.

Hegai, the king's chamberlain, set his eyes on Esther, and she found favour. By virtue of his office as King Xerxes' gatekeeper, he was uniquely positioned to help accelerate the chances of any of the maidens in the harem. As the Scriptures showed, he graciously lavished Esther with that extra edge she needed.

There is every possibility she might have been given special oils, perfumes and cosmetics that were not generally available. She also had a special designated meal which must have, in no small measure, aided her chances of enhancing her beauty and physical attributes according to the king's elevated taste. This, again, could only have been got through the knowledge of the king's chamberlain.

Even without getting to the palace and becoming queen, favour ensured she was bestowed with seven attendants from the palace, who were responsible for attending to her every need. Apart from this, she was given the choicest apartment within the harem to guarantee her comfort. It is little wonder that this was recorded:

> *"Now the King was more attracted to Esther*
> *more than to any of the other women, and she*
> *won his favour and approval more than any of*
> *the other virgins. So he set a royal crown upon*
> *her head and made her king instead of Vashti."*
> Esther 2:17 (NIV)

Proverbs 3:4 talks about winning favour and a good name in the sight of God and man (with the precondition of not letting love and faithfulness ever leave us—that is, to bind them around our necks, and write them on the tablets of our hearts).

Therefore, the first major principle you must undertake to win over gatekeepers is attracting the divine favour of God, which facilitates favour before men. This will navigate the hearts of men towards your desire, and you will become pleasing to whoever sets their eyes on you.

Esther experienced it with her own gatekeeper, Hegai, and it also ensured she found favour before King Xerxes. In many years gone by, I flouted this principle, thereby resting on my personal perceived prowess, and I paid dearly for my ignorance. God is willing to ensure you are clothed in His favour that will make gatekeepers advance your desire and cause. Esther paid no amount to Hegai, yet she was privileged to be personally prepared by the chief courtier himself for no just reason other than favour.

You will find yourself navigating the maze of men easier with the favour of the Almighty upon your life. The favour of God, as stated in Psalm 90:17, establishes the work of our hands, so there is a place for hard work and another level of its establishment by the favour that comes from only the Almighty.

Therefore, finding favour and good repute, as stated in Proverbs 3:4, is a prerequisite in handling not just gatekeepers, but also all men. The foundation of the access you desire must be built on divine favour that guarantees not just supernatural ease, but also an acceleration that will leave many shocked. Do you need access to the king? Seek favour first, and you are guaranteed that Hegai will bend the rules in your favour, ultimately ensuring that you wear the crown. This was true thousands of years ago and is still in operation this very day. You must unashamedly desire and seek favour to guarantee your success.

BE DISCERNING

Discernment is the ability to see things (people also) for what they really are and not for what you want them to be. On the contrary, many of us often want to perceive people in a certain way that doesn't reflect their true identities.

The need to obtain the grace to discern gatekeepers is a very important principle. Many times, we often lose the opportunity to gain access to new levels of success based on our inability to discern individuals that cross our paths. Oftentimes, these individuals do not appear with a tag or on a billboard announcing their ability to be bridges or ladders to your next level. The individuals who seek to ascend new heights and who require access to the hearts of men always have their mental antennae permanently tuned to the station of discernment.

One of the major hacks in achieving this, which I have optimized in my own personal dealings, is by putting everyone on the same level of importance. This eliminates the risk of downplaying the importance of any individual that may turn out to be a gatekeeper. This hack, therefore, guarantees without fail that I don't fall foul of this key principle.

Oftentimes, gatekeepers or men who tend to be helpers may not appear the way you expect; you may not necessarily meet them at their stations of influence when you see or interact with them. I have had the privilege of undeniable access to great men and women by simply discerning certain individuals who I perceived had the gift of access. Sometimes, I "bank" those individuals in my mental bank and "withdraw" when the season of their needs/relevance arises for them.

John 7:24 (NIV) says, "*Stop judging by mere appearances, but instead judge correctly.*" This is a strong admonition to stop using our physical eyes which gaze only at the surface, but to use the eyes of our spirits to make key decisions on who we should and shouldn't bother interacting with. Sometimes, the discernment may not be by seeing but, instead, by hearing. This is done by cherry-picking what is said to you by individuals, which may reveal clues that can be used to your advantage.

In all your interactions with fellow men, you will meet all kinds of people. It is often said you are one person away from everybody else, showing you how interconnected the human race is. Nevertheless, all that connection is premised on the ability to discern men in proximity and from a distance.

Charles R. Swindoll, an American evangelical preacher, would say, "*We all need discernment in what we see and what we hear and what we believe.*" By man's construct, our natural eyes tend to be the judge and jury when it comes to the mental impression of the men we come in contact with; and, as expected, the result is almost always a flawed judgement or conclusion.

The need to understand the importance of all men and discern that each human carries a potential key to open a vault we all seek to open is a powerful insight for daily living. Many individuals capable of propelling your acceleration come in unexpected garments. As such, the seeking out of this unique gift of discernment is one we must adopt if we are to deal effectively with gatekeepers. Psalm 119:16 says, *"Teach me good discernment and knowledge…"* This clearly indicates that good discernment can be learnt, and you shouldn't hesitate to have God teach you how to discern people aright.

STUDY YOUR TARGET WHEN KNOWN

Studying your targeted gatekeeper when known and the ability to get into the mind of the gatekeeper to understand how they function are key principles to winning over any gatekeeper. One of my favourite authors of all time is the amazing British theologian C.S. Lewis who once famously remarked that, *"Friendship is born at that moment when one person says to another: 'What! You too? I thought I was the only one."*

Individuals who overcome the high hurdles of men are those who, through formal or informal means, have attained unprecedented levels of mastery in the demanding study of the complex human nature. The greatest gift any man can give himself is an intentional, lifetime study of his fellow human beings. You are always going to be at a disadvantage when you go into a room blindfolded, without performing due diligence on a gatekeeper.

Let me borrow an analogy we can all relate to. Have you watched one of those National Geographic Wild programmes and seen certain animals with reptilian metabolism, which can spend days studying their prey before they strike? We must adopt a similar real-life skill of patience in studying those who guard access points.

What kind of personality traits do they possess intrinsically? What makes them tick? What are their upsides and downsides? What temperaments and behavioural attributes do they possess? What are their likes or dislikes? What views shape their mindsets which, in turn, reveal their philosophies/ideologies that can affect your access?

The right answers to the above questions will put you in an advantageous position to approach gatekeepers and build lifetime relationships to your benefit. By creating real conversations and not just empty conversations of enquiry, you are potentially able to open a book of revelation into the mind and life of your target. Certain common mental meeting points will breed trust and inevitably lower existing walls of defences against individuals who seek to always penetrate the same.

Knowing the power of sports, I have, in many instances, used the love of a particular sport or team to gain access to the hearts of so many gatekeepers simply by studying my target. This could also be achieved through shared hobbies, interests, desires, etc.

This principle must become a way of life for you due to the immense power it possesses. Through a study, over time, I have come to the conclusion that everyone must, at certain intervals, reveal a hidden combination or, at least, offer clues that open the padlocks of their lives. It is left for you to pick the locks after they are within your grasp.

If you want to win over a gatekeeper, then learn to study such a person first in close proximity, or put in the work to do some research if you are at a distance. Better still, you can contract someone to conduct such research for you. You can seek out individuals who know such gatekeepers and gather valuable data on what it would take to get access. By taking this principle to heart, you will realize the revelation of actions you can then execute to gain the favour you desire. You must possess a genuine knowledge of them, adapt accordingly, and move on to the next principle.

Unfortunately, many are lazy in their approach to gatekeepers; they are often hasty and hardly strategic. Proverbs 19:2 describes it in a succinct way: *"It isn't good to have zeal without knowledge; nor being hasty with one's feet and missing the way."* To win gatekeepers, take the time and pay the dues of researching them properly before making an approach like a predator, otherwise you may miss the way.

BUILD STRATEGIC AND INTENTIONAL RELATIONSHIPS

Building strategic and intentional relationships with gatekeepers is a masterpiece in the puzzle of life and business. Unfortunately, it is one of the most ignored principles in winning over any man, especially gatekeepers.

The nugget in this principle, which lies at the very heart of it, is that *"strategic relationships are real wealth."* The kind of relationships being referenced here is not the typical self-seeking type, but the selfless type that seeks mutual benefits for all parties involved. In other words, it should not be a selfish or parasitic version, but a symbiotic relationship with a targeted gatekeeper.

The reality is no one likes a user, but everyone appreciates individuals that practise the art of investing their time, resources and efforts in building something that is sustainable. Every time you engage this principle, imagine the sights of light-filled skyscrapers anywhere in the four corners of the earth. The admiration they all command is a testament to the unseen foundations that have been established to carry such an enviable weight of steel and concrete.

The law of relationships is further emphasized in the divine commandment given to man in the book of Genesis 1:28 (NIV): *"Be fruitful and multiply…"* This was clearly a charge for man to be "relational" because everything on the earth involving men advances, increases, multiplies, and is done on the basis of strategic relationships. Relationships are rightfully described as advantageous connections, and the easiest way to win gatekeepers in your bid to rise and succeed in life is clearly through building your foundation on this tested and timeless platform.

Also, due to the fact that strategic relationships are a more superior currency that can be used to purchase almost anything we need in our lives, including access, they are, therefore, one the most potent arrows in your quiver to win a gatekeeper. Many make the mistake of believing money is the only thing that can be used to purchase access. Although it is important, money is limited in its potency. Thus, you can use relationships to get you through almost any door. Some individuals owe their own access to the spouse of an individual, a domestic member of staff or just about anyone.

Amos 3:3 enquires, *"Can two work together except they be agreed?"* This Scripture highlights the important component needed in human dealings, which is agreement—a further expression of strategic relationships. You must, therefore, be intentional about building strategic and intentional relationships so you can work in tandem with others to bring success to your life and business.

LEAN ON THEIR VALUABLE KNOWLEDGE & INSIGHT

Now, you have successfully navigated the landmines and gained visibility before the gatekeeper. Many, at this stage, are like a deer staring into the headlamps of a vehicle on a lonely highway, unsure of whether to run or stay. So, what do you do at this stage of confusion when you have one or both feet across the door? Let's quickly revisit the story of Queen Esther to extract some nectar regarding the principle of understanding the invaluable knowledge gatekeepers embody for your benefit.

Esther 2:13 (NIV) states that, *"And this is how she would go to the king: **Anything she wanted was given to her to take with her** from the harem to the king's palace."* (Emphasis mine)

It was a prerequisite that any of the maidens who were to go in to meet King Xeres, the mighty ruler of Persia, was to take along a gift which, in my humble assessment, would speak volumes of their personalities to compliment the earlier described beauty and transformation they had undergone in the past year. But we are offered a powerful tool in the arsenal of Esther, one that set her apart and over other maidens seeking to win the king's heart, as stated below:

*"When the turn came for Esther (the young woman
Mordecai had adopted, the daughter of his uncle Abihail)
to go to the king, **she asked for nothing other than
what Hegai, the king's eunuch who was in charge of
the harem, suggested.** And Esther won the favour
of everyone who saw her."*
Esther 2:16 (NIV), emphasis mine

The secret weapon deployed by Esther, after gaining favour from the gatekeeper, was to lean on his valuable knowledge and insight into what would please the king. She did not lean on her understanding, belief or wishful thinking of what she perceived King Xerxes would like.

Many struggle at this stage because there exists a preconceived notion of what they would like to do when it comes to engaging with the gatekeeper. Regardless of your plans, you must understand that no one knows better than the man who mans the gate. He is privy to information, routines and preferences, and such intimate personal details are invaluable when maximized. Your actions suddenly become magical in nature. Better still, you will be reverenced as possessing an inner eye into what pleases your ultimate target. Ignoring this principle and fixing your gaze only on your target will guarantee your travel towards your goal at an agonizingly slow pace. This will be really painful, especially when there is the option of leveraging information that will give you turbo speed.

Individuals who understand this principle have gone to access kings, presidents, CEOs, spiritual leaders and about anyone of significance and repute. They achieved the same by optimizing valuable knowledge that was easily got via interactions with gatekeepers around them.

It is your responsibility to go all out and possess vital insights and then go on to utilize them to great effect. Learn to lean on those closest to your targets. While writing this chapter, I was reflecting on a particular potential client whose gatekeeper happens to be his driver. The driver approached me to offer vital information on how I can propose my value to the organization he works for, even offering to go the extra mile of constantly reminding his principal on the outstanding proposal I had offered. I am positive about adding value to that organization because I decided to lean on the valuable knowledge and insight of that gatekeeper.

Many push aside such gatekeepers in the grand scheme of their approach. In the process, they lose the most important part of winning an individual over.

PATIENCE AND RESISTING THE URGE TO OVER-REQUEST

*"Some of our greatest blessings
come with patience."*
Warren Wiersbe

Gatekeepers are, in most instances, constantly bombarded by innumerable requests that take a huge toll on them. So, to truly maximize the relationship with a gatekeeper, you must possess the often sidelined trait of patience. This is not an easy attribute to own and walk in. In some instances, I have reaped from the seeds of patience many years after the first contact, when such may have been forgotten by others. Patience gives you an enviable and desirable personality; it bestows on you a perceived air of control that is attractive to any gatekeeper guarding any realm of influence or personality you seek. Often, its absence leads many down the path of missed blessings. Indeed, impatience can be costly when it comes to handling gatekeepers.

You will realize that when you lack patience, you will constitute a nuisance to such gatekeepers who, in turn, will shut off the oxygen valve of the relationship you seek to build. For this reason, you must resist the urge to appear too anxious for what you seek to get. Imbibe a gentle, mature and infectious disposition in your dealings, and I can assure you this disarms even the most difficult gatekeepers. It is irresistible to almost any man. Be like the duck gliding on the pond with grace and poise, but furiously kicking under the water.

When it appears you are making no progress, the first impulse is to throw in the towel. Conceding to defeat can, however, be averted by demonstrating patience. It reveals a lot about not just ourselves but others as well. It is why patience is referred to as the companion of wisdom.

Another major turn-off is the urge to make all your requests all at once, otherwise called over-requesting. There is a need, during your preparation stage, to be methodological in what exactly you want. That is, you must learn how to present your requests in a sequential manner. You must resist the urge to be like everyone else, who sees an open door as a one-off opportunity. Those who are patient and methodological have the unique advantage of always returning for more.

Patience fertilizes trust faster than many other qualities. It also scans and reveals motives. The truth is most gatekeepers are naturally suspicious, and much more to desperate individuals. Therefore, you must reveal your sincere intention to be around for the very long haul. You must be genuinely seen as intending to nurture mutually beneficial relationships and not be like others who seek a "fling".

Most gatekeepers are comparable to onions: these individuals possess several protective layers. Patience will, therefore, be needed to peel through each layer to reach your goal. With patience, you must endure the tears, sacrifices and discomfort each layer of peeling presents.

BE PREPARED

Preparation is always a forerunner or indicator of seriousness; it is a revelation of the character you truly possess. The Webster Dictionary defines it as *"the action or process of preparing or being prepared for use or consideration"*.

The latter part of that definition is instructive: the preparation is for use or consideration. In spite of the timing or opportunity for when you may have to make that presentation, or when you have the desired access, what is expected of you is preparation. Many have had the opportunity to make elevator pitches to gatekeepers with no notice; the ability to deliver on your feet can make or break all you have dreamed of your entire life. So, it pays to be prepared. I have made my pitches at weddings, children's parties, shopping mall car parks, barber shops, banking halls, etc. You can take your cue from me by being always ready to forge a new alliance.

The quote of Whitney M. Young Jnr., an American civil rights leader, on preparation is apt: *"It's better to be prepared for an opportunity and not have one, than to have an opportunity and not be prepared."* If you truly want to gain access and win over a gatekeeper, a major task you owe yourself is preparation. Cover every possible base, do your research and, importantly, know what you want and be prepared to communicate that desire in any environment and circumstance. Practise your short pitches, have vital documents within sight and be appropriately dressed as you approach that gatekeeper to introduce yourself and further engage him.

Most gatekeepers do not possess the patience to stomach unpreparedness when access is sought. As such, you must sidetrack other individuals on the corridor of waiting, with your hunger to hit the nail on the head when the occasion presents itself. Many have met gatekeepers during airline flights, airport terminals, social events, religious settings, etc. Sometimes, it may be a chance encounter or introduction, but regardless of the location or circumstances that birthed it, preparation is the key that will open the door on the spot. With that in mind, you must always be ready to give a good account of yourself at a moment's notice to win over a gatekeeper.

THE POWER OF LANGUAGE AND THE IMPORTANCE OF COMMUNICATION

The power of communicating appropriately and effectively is a major key in winning over a gatekeeper. After a careful study of this individual, you must possess the much-needed language prowess and effective body gestures that communicate your intent and desire to gain access.

While a few paragraphs will definitely not do justice to this principle, there is a need to invest in building yourself effectively with powerful tools that will communicate your feelings in an attractive manner. There are certain words that must be present in your communication library that pass across the key values such as honour, respect, integrity, wisdom, discipline and diligence. This will inevitably put you at the forefront and implant you in the subconscious mind of the gatekeeper you seek to win over.

This is especially true in a world where morals and seamless communication of age-old values are fast eroding and replaced by new "societal norms" that are lacking value. You will be adjudged as someone that can be trusted when you communicate effectively and respectfully. The skills you possess must mirror the above-mentioned timeless values, while attention and care must also be accorded to the other side of the coin: nonverbal communication through the use of gestures. Age-old behavioural traits such as courtesy should not be downplayed to any degree. They come in handy when separating the wheat from the chaff of individuals seeking access. You must make sure all your gestures also communicate honour, first for the gatekeeper as an individual and, next, for the office he or she occupies, before even the person, system or structure you seek access to.

In Colossians 4:6 (NIV), the Scriptures give us a major illumination on the power of our words by saying, *"Let your conversation be always full of grace, seasoned with salt, so that you may know how to answer everyone."* You must understand that the same flavour that salt provides, which stimulates taste, is similar in nature to the words that proceed from our mouths. When communicating with gatekeepers, ensure your words bring flavour within the hearing of the listener.

Due to the fact that your interactions with the gatekeepers are premised on the persuasion to gain access, Proverbs 16:23 (NLT) says that, *"From a wise mind comes wise speech; the words of the wise are persuasive."* You must learn the act of disseminating wise words because such words are laced with the power of persuasion, which is a major key to winning gatekeepers and gaining access.

Good communication, like most other skills, can be learnt. There is a treasure trove of materials available for any individual willing to imbibe studying individuals who are the epitome of excellent communication. It is vital because you must communicate your desires to men.

LEARN HOW TO MAKE THE GATEKEEPER FEEL IMPORTANT

"Kind words are like honey...," says Proverbs 16:24 (NIV). Nothing is more pleasing to a man, especially a gatekeeper, than kind words which the Bible likens to honey. Your ability to use your words to great effect, by showering praises when necessary, is a key element in having fruitful relationships with all men.

As mentioned in the previous chapter, your ability to express honour with the use of words is a game changer in any human relationship, especially when such words are powered by honesty. Doing so has a lasting, unexplainable effect on the recipient—the gatekeeper.

In Proverbs 18:20 (NIV), King Solomon had this to say about the power and effect of words: *"Words satisfy the soul as food satisfies the stomach; the right words on a person's lips bring satisfaction."* This insight is a powerful indicator highlighting the importance of words by putting it on a par with one of man's basic necessities: food. Well-cooked words carry a similar impact as the satisfaction a well-cooked meal brings to one's stomach.

There is a need to master the use of wise speech to make not just gatekeepers but also all men feel important because, by nature, man is inherently cautious. Your speech must be powered by wisdom because it carries a more potent force than you can imagine; it is more valuable than any gemstone you can think of.

If you want to gain access, learn how to make the gatekeepers feel important with your words; shower praise and generous appreciation on them, and reap the rewards therein.

Showing constant kindness through words can accomplish much more than you can possibly imagine. According to Albert Schweitzer, "As the sun melts ice, kindness causes misunderstanding, mistrust and hostility to evaporate." Our words can be like "golden apples set in silver when spoken at the right time" (Proverbs 25:11).

If you want to win a gatekeeper over, learn how to make them feel important with the use of choice words at the right time. Learn to caution yourself because words, which cannot return to your mouth when uttered, can make or break gatekeepers' impression of you.

BRING VALUE
TO THE TABLE

Value is defined as the usefulness and importance of something or someone. Simply put, it is best described as an indicator of worth. I am referring to that which connotes a superior offering or quality, which you intend to provide and which will be critically assessed by the gatekeeper.

Value distinguishes people; it draws a line between you and others in the queue, who are seeking the same access. Value is a golden crown that cannot be ignored or passed over. Success in life is heavily reliant on value, so you must be ready to prove to the gatekeeper that you can bring value to the table (remember, always, that you are not the only one seeking what you desire). Your ability to present your contributions with uniqueness, originality and excellence will make you more acceptable by any gatekeeper and potentially open the door of greatness.

Our very existence in the world itself is built on value; you must, therefore, begin to articulate and go on to establish your value proposition to win over any gatekeeper.

Due to the fact that real value naturally births influence, which is a forerunner of relevance, there must be an intentional act of building up your intrinsic value, ensuring that it serves not just mere men but also kings. If your value is at the level of a 5-star Michelin Chef, there is every possibility you will serve the greats of this age; but if your value is of roadside quality, you have already defined your audience and may not proceed past many gates. While value can be multifaceted, at its core still lies the same proposal of exceeding the expectations of others.

An author and speaker Bernard Clive had this to say about value: *"The world pays no attention to those who have nothing to offer."* The understanding of this will help to chaperone your interpersonal relationships, especially with gatekeepers whose disposition is geared towards knowing why you should be considered. Are you only interested in taking and adding nothing? You must consider that, in any sphere of influence, certain relationship fatigue will automatically set in if a relationship is one-sided.

Let me state this fact here and now: there are certain individuals you will never have access to until you become a person of value. Value is like a big tag placed on you with the bold inscription "pick me".

Notably, there are essential steps in becoming a person of value. First, you must recognize your God-given gifts/abilities. Next, you must continuously pursue development and make no excuses for mediocrity. Also, you must be a reliable problem solver.

The story of Joseph in the book of Genesis is a "locus classicus" (borrowing a phrase from my legal background, meaning an authority on a subject matter) on the power of value.

Joseph was one of the 12 sons of Jacob, one of the patriarchs of the Christian faith, and Scripture records that his father Jacob loved him more than his other brothers. This was further exemplified by the gift of the coloured cloak Joseph received from his father, further infuriating his already agitated brothers, who were already taken aback by the preference and then the gift of dreams of the talkative youngster. All of this pointed to certain superiority over his older brothers, thus leading to destructive jealousy that would consume them and be the catalyst for our story.

The fire of jealousy in their bellies would lead to the brothers selling Joseph into slavery; he would be taken to Egypt, and he eventually became a steward to Potiphar, one of Pharaoh's chief officers. Unfortunately, an unholy admiration by Potiphar's wife would lead him to more trouble: he was accused of attempted rape despite his exemplary leadership and value to the household, and he ended up in jail.

In Genesis 40, Joseph encountered gatekeepers who, at the time, did not appear as such. Pharaoh's chief cup-bearer and chief baker had offended their master, and both ended up in prison where Joseph was. They were assigned to him, and he looked after them. While in jail, they both had dreams that were correctly interpreted by Joseph; the fulfilment of his

Godly interpretations would lead to the chief cup-bearer being restored to his position of access to the most powerful man in all of Egypt and the chief baker losing his head.

This gatekeeper, though after a considerable time of not giving the young Joseph in the prison any thought, would remember the young Hebrew man of value when his master Pharaoh demanded a man who would interpret two troubling dreams he had, for which he could get no answer even from his own magicians. In Genesis 41:12 (NIV), the cup-bearer would say, *"Now a young Hebrew was there with us, a servant of the captain of the guard. We told him our dreams, and he interpreted them for us, giving each man the interpretation of his dream."*

The gatekeeper remembered the value Joseph possessed; this proposition to the king would ensure that Joseph bypassed government protocol and bureaucracy to stand before Pharaoh in record time. This is an attainment which one may be tempted to conclude would be impossible for a foreign slave.

Joseph would go on to further justify the golden access given by this gatekeeper by displaying his God-given ability to interpret the dreams, and not just stop there but add further value with unexpected recommendations without a prompt.

"Therefore Pharaoh should find
an intelligent and wise man and put
him in charge of the entire land of Egypt."
Genesis 41:33 (NIV)

His suggestions were so well received that, on that day, he was appointed to be in charge of the court and country with only Pharaoh having a rank higher than his in all of Egypt.

So, while you may not possess the gifts of dream interpretation like Joseph, you are not, by any measure, lacking what you can present to your own gatekeeper to gain a royal invite to the courts of Pharaoh.

It is, therefore, imperative that you are a person of value—you should have something to be brought to the table even after you have been granted an audience. You may not get any prior notice about when you will be ordered to shave, change your clothes and appear before the one you seek, so be prepared to show your value whether you are in prison or the palace.

SHOW CONTINUOUS APPRECIATION

Abraham Harold Maslow, an American psychologist, is popular for creating the Hierarchy of Needs, which is a theory of psychological health predicated on fulfilling innate human needs according to priority. This culminated in self-actualization and completely revolutionized the study of human nature.

One of the highlights of his research is that the highest psychological need of man is the need to be loved, accepted, celebrated and "appreciated".

The use of continuous, sincere appreciation is a powerful tool in winning over any gatekeeper. You must constantly remember that relationships do not maintain themselves, and you have the ability to programme goodness which you can then send to your future to await you.

A major error many commit is waiting for rewards to come to them first before employing this principle in their dealings with others and, then, they wonder why they have never proceeded beyond their mental expectations.

At this point, I must put out a disclaimer: am I advocating underhanded dealings or encouraging unscriptural vices that are heavily frowned upon, such as giving bribes? Not at all! Rather, I am encouraging employing one of the most basic human relationship principles which Scripture supports, and that is showing appreciation to others in every way we can without necessarily expecting anything in return. Weaning yourself off any expectation helps you grow and nurture a genuine relationship that could feed you and generations for decades to come.

When you show generosity with your time, and you give resources with gratitude and praise, you place yourself in pole position to be at the frontal lobe of your gatekeeper's brain; and it is only natural that they easily remember you when the opportunity presents itself.

Sadly, some individuals, despite their amazing skills and their value propositions, struggle to gain access because they fail at this hurdle. Learning to use gifts to win gatekeepers, not in a brash, manipulative manner, but in a strategic and intentional way is vital because it is biblical in nature and very powerful. What you can gift is up to you; it can be time, relationship, attention and so forth.

The Bible says in Proverbs 18:16 (NLT) that, *"Giving a gift can open doors; it gives access to important people!"* It's there in black and white that your giving affords you access to important people. So, you must, from today, start giving what you can. Look out for important dates and milestones in the lives of gatekeepers, and celebrate them. You can bless them with a material gift or even condole with them in moments of grief. In fact, the latter, in my humble opinion, carries a seed that can birth a massive harvest in the long run. People may forget those who celebrated them during the good times, but I assure you that they hardly forget those who were with them during their worst days.

Appreciation is, therefore, a door opener regardless of the thick density of the door you are knocking on and the size of the gatekeeper overseeing entry. This principle is applicable to all men without a single exception.

BE HUMBLE

Quite a number of individuals seem to have disjointed views of what humility truly means; let me help put it in perspective. Humility is not thinking less of yourself; it is thinking of yourself less. Humility is thinking more of others.

Humility is a sine qua non (an essential condition; a thing that is absolutely necessary) when it comes to gatekeepers, and pride (being rebellious; the opposite of humility) is a major turn-off that will make you miss out on the best of life due to its very selfish disposition that makes up its DNA.

Pride is a high or inordinate opinion of one's dignity, merit or superiority over others, whether as cherished in the mind or displayed in conduct.

Pride brings disgrace, but humility comes with wisdom; displaying pride to gatekeepers can only lead to having doors of opportunities routinely slammed in your face. There is hardly anywhere pride is mentioned with rising and acceptability by others. It's usually referenced with ruin and regrets. It can be both vocal and represented in conduct, and it is a venom that one must resist with every fibre of one's being.

To get ahead in the quest for a better life, you must think more of others and, almost automatically, you will become more attractive to people around you. Then, you can have your requests met eagerly and desirably.

Scripture is rife with provisions encouraging us to be humble and identifying it as a prerequisite due to its lifting power in the affairs of men. Ephesians 4:2 (NIV) advises that we should be completely humble and gentle. I Peter 5:5 (NIV) speaks about adorning oneself with humility thus: *"All of you, clothe yourselves with humility toward one another, because God opposes the proud but shows favour to the humble."*

Humility must precede your receiving an honour. Therefore, to receive the honour of access from a gatekeeper, you must be humble.

PRACTISE HONOUR

"If you want to gain access, honour is the key."
Dr David Ogbueli,
Nigerian Preacher, Teacher, Author

The inability of one man to show honour to the gatekeepers to a future king of Israel almost cost him his life at first, while his wife's display of honour secured her future. David was anointed to be the chosen leader of God's own people, the Israelites, after the rejection of Saul due to pride and disobedience. David and his band of soldiers were on the run from Saul who sought their necks, leading them to become fugitives living off the benevolence of others and making caves their habitation.

The band of misfits moved towards the wilderness of Maon, where a wealthy but crude and mean man called Nabal lived with his wife Abigail. David, upon realizing the comfort of this man, would have his men (gatekeepers) approach him for any provisions he might share. He sneered and remarked about why he should help outlaws, forgetting that they had protected his servants and sheep, and never allowed them to experience harm or theft. The gatekeepers took the message back to their leader David who vowed to shed blood for the insult.

On the other hand, his wife Abigail, upon being informed by a servant about the dishonour displayed by her husband (see I Samuel 25:18, NIV) and understanding the gravity of the dishonour shown, knew there would be trouble for the whole household. She would quickly instruct for provisions to be prepared and taken by her servant ahead of her to meet David and his men, without informing her husband.

She would later meet David on her way, getting off her donkey, bowing low and declaring, *"I accept all blame in this matter, my lord."* She would describe her husband this way: *"I know Nabal is a wicked and ill-tempered man; please don't pay any attention to him. He is a fool, just as his name suggests."* The most important declaration she would make, thereby appreciating the role of gatekeepers, is this: *"But I never even saw the young men you sent."*

Abigail would go on to honour David, acknowledge his battles and would conclude by saying, *"When the Lord has done the great things He has promised you, please remember me, your servant!"* David would acknowledge her wisdom and assured her no harm would come to her husband or any of his men.

In verse 36 of the same chapter, when Abigail arrived home, she found that Nabal was throwing a big party, celebrating like a king, and was very drunk. As such, she didn't tell him anything about her meeting with David until dawn the next day. As a result of breaking the news to him, he had a stroke and lay paralyzed on his bed like a stone. He would go on to die in 10 days' time.

As for Abigail who understood how badly the gatekeepers to King David were treated, upon hearing about the death of Nabal, she sent messengers to ask her to become his wife. To justify this decision, when the messengers informed her, she bowed low to the ground and responded, *"I, your servant, would be happy to marry David. I would be even willing to become a slave, washing the feet of his servants."*

Abigail understood the need to always show honour to those who stand before people of influence and power; she recognized how badly the gatekeepers were treated with the insult meted out to them by her foolish husband. She quickly remedied the situation and ensured that, in the end, she became one of the wives of Israel's most powerful king. By contrast, Nabal's folly cost him his life and wife.

There is not a single man/woman guarding access, who likes or tolerates dishonour; many individuals make elementary errors of judgement by looking down on these individuals without realizing that the feedback these gatekeepers give kings makes all the difference.

No man has the vaccination against honour, so communicate with respect and a purpose, and you will, without a shadow of doubt, keep the gatekeepers on your side and win over the kings.

STOOP TO CONQUER

One tool that I have found very useful is the peripatetic effect which is often a way of asking the gatekeeper for advice on something that interests you, in such a way that you will get them interested and invested in it. This is achieved by stooping to conquer which is to adopt a role, position, attitude, behaviour, undertaking, etc. that is seen as being beneath one's abilities or social position in order to achieve one's end.

Conceding to the insider knowledge of a gatekeeper is of the utmost importance such that it cannot be overstated. Many gatekeepers may appear to be "lower" than you expect, socially speaking. In some instances, some could be uneducated; on other occasions, they may be rude in speech and mannerisms. Nevertheless, you must never forget that even a king who reigns over subjects must, at the start of his reign, bow his head to have a crown placed on it by a lesser mortal.

Many, on a daily basis, are losing vital life-changing opportunities due to the inability to swallow their pride. It is a principle of life that, to gain something, we often have to give something in return. The price of giving up your pride in exchange for your desire is a fair bargain.

Resist the temptation to always show yourself or appear to be too knowledgeable; it's often repulsive to most gatekeepers. There is a line between appearing smart/confident and pushing things down the throats of others to appear well schooled.

Learn to stoop and ask for clarifications even when, in some instances, you presume to have answers already. Just like in ancient times, you cannot sidestep gatekeepers to gain access in modern times. Therefore, you must adopt a submissive role, which you might not be accustomed to, but can be learnt.

You must learn to take a position that is aligned with that of the gatekeeper even if it's for the time being; you cannot be seen to take a solitary stance that puts the gatekeeper on the opposite side of a table.

There are also certain attitudes that must support your position, mostly in your mannerisms; always bear in mind that a large chunk of our communication as human beings is non-verbal in nature. You may have to engage in certain undertakings that you naturally may consider beneath you, but this is vital to stooping. Often, some gatekeepers may seek to test individuals to enable them sieve such people's true intentions.

Put aside your abilities, especially if they will appear to subsume that of the gatekeeper you need. Seek their truth, acknowledge it and run with it; trust me, it pays dividends in the long run.

LET THEM SHINE ALWAYS

Man possesses an inherent and often silent desire to be in the spotlight—it is a trait we all seem to have carried into adulthood from our childhood, and you must be ready to concede that ground to a gatekeeper. These unique individuals must be given due acknowledgement at all times, whether they desire it or not. The temptation to shift the luminous light from their position to yours may well short-circuit a growing or even established relationship. Always allow the gatekeeper to shine and take the praise even when they may resist what they could term unwarranted and undeserved attention. Let the shine return to the source of the privileged information, access and favour at all times.

I have seen many in business falter at this hurdle, and they struggle to return to the scene of their earlier victory to repeat similar successes. This is due to the fact that the gatekeeper was mistreated. Ironically, such a gatekeeper may not be able to pinpoint what has silently triggered their new resentment towards a previous recipient of their goodness. You probably have unconsciously triggered a silent alarm, which doesn't blare out loud sounds but has passed sufficient information to its owner to be wary of whoever triggered it and take possible future action against him or her.

If you desire to win a gatekeeper over, you must ensure he is always the centre of attraction. Be wise enough to remain in the shadows, and allow the gatekeepers to be the one to usher you into the blinding light of attraction where you take the applause of gaining access and achieving the goals you set out to achieve.

ABOUT THE AUTHOR

Chris Omoijiade, in one word, is a multipotentialite. He is a Speaker, Coach, Author, Trainer, Lawyer, Entrepreneur and, most significantly, a Minister of the Gospel.

The Dean of Value Creation possesses 17 years' experience across entrepreneurship, law, professional public speaking, business mentorship and consultancy.

Through the Chris Omoijiade Company, he is transforming thousands of individuals and businesses every year, globally, across various platforms and mountains of influence.

He holds law degrees from the University of Lagos, Nigeria, and the University of Hertfordshire, United Kingdom. He is an alumnus of the Koinonia School of Ministry Abuja Campus and the New Generation Bible Training Institute (an expression of the Sword of the Spirit Ministries, Ibadan, Nigeria). Also, he holds a Diploma in Theology from the RCN Theological Seminary, Adullam, Makurdi, Benue State, Nigeria and a current student of Rhema Bible School, Nigeria.

Chris is the Author of the well-received book "Get Ahead – Practical Steps to Face Life's Realities and Embrace Success" and several e-books and online courses.

He is also a serial philanthropist and unshakable optimist in the possibilities that the human spirit possesses.

He is happily married to Oduola-Chris Omoijiade, and they are blessed with two amazing sons Eromosele and Ethan, tools in the hands of the Almighty God.

He travels around the world extensively on assignments to impact the world positively but still calls the city of Lagos, Nigeria, home.

ABOUT THE CHRIS OMOIJIADE COMPANY

The Chris Omoijiade company, formerly known as "Attrium Consultants", is a leadership, management and boutique innovative consultancy firm that is rededicated to effective operation, administration and implementation of educational programmes and tools aimed at enhancing productivity for individuals, corporate entities and the public sector.

We achieve this by developing in-house practical approaches and solutions to solving life and business problems. We also operate under licence from some of the world's leading authorities on various fields of knowledge dissemination to ensure growth and profitability.

We achieve all these through various pathways and platforms, including speaking, mentoring, training, coaching and consultancy.

To book Chris for your speaking engagements, consulting, company keynote addresses, trainings, and for ministrations, you can use any of the channels below:

- +234 908 123 0000
- admin@tcocglobal.com
- Chris@chrisomoijiade.com
- ceo@tcocglobal.com

Follow on social media

- chrisomoijiade
- chrisomoijiade
- @tcocglobal
- @arimathea_believers_network
- chrisomoijiade
- christopher Omoijiade
- The Chris Omoijiade Company
- www.chrisomoijiade.com
- www.tcocglobal.com
- www.arimatheanetwork.org
- comoijiade